Seventy Swaying Palms

Relevant, Inspirational Poetry for Everyone

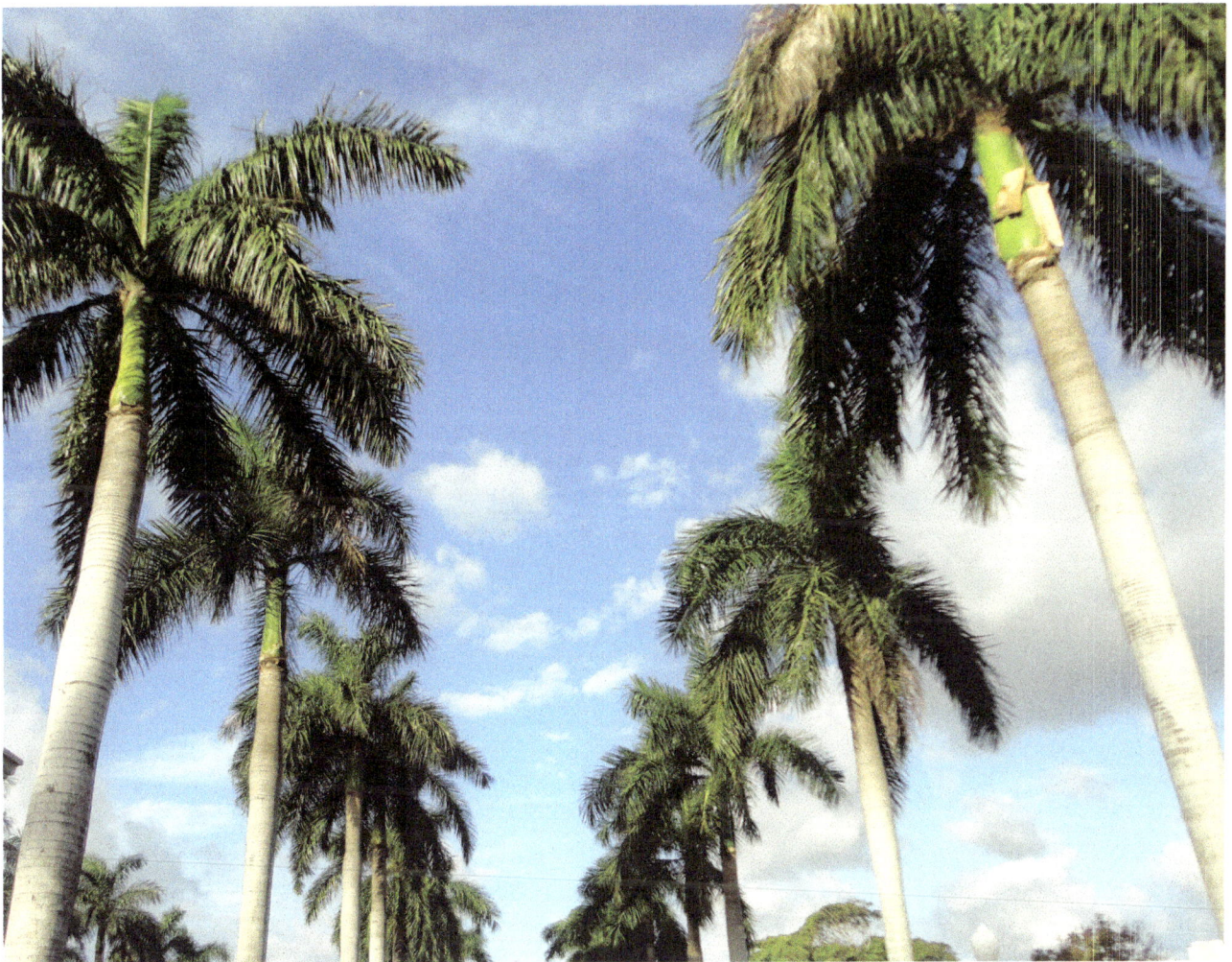

IRENE ROORDA

Irene

ISBN 978-1-64028-944-4 (Paperback)
ISBN 978-1-64028-946-8 (Hard Cover)
ISBN 978-1-64028-945-1 (Digital)

Christian Faith Publishing, Inc.
296 Chestnut Street
Meadville, PA 16335
www.christianfaithpublishing.com

All scripture verses were taken from the King James version of the Bible.

Printed in the United States of America

Contents

Part VI: Feminine Reflections

Part VII: Death's Painful Separation

Part VIII: Bitter Anguish through Fiery Trials

Part IX: Hopeful Encouragement and Inspiration

Part X: Perspectives on Present-Day Issues

Part XI: Life's Fleeting Beauty

Introduction

My husband, Paul and I have resided in Palm Beach Gardens, Florida, for the last forty years. The Lord has blessed us with four wonderful children and now, two dynamic grandsons. It was when our talented second son, Caleb lost his battle with depression, that I discovered writing poetry was therapeutic.

Poetry acts like the spigot of the soul that splashes out sparkling joy from the sunlight of God's love; as well as spewing pain, from the rusty pipes of this life's ugly realities. Soothing to our oozing wounds, as well as strangling in a throat-grip of emotion, it embraces the whole spectrum of sentiments that color our earthly journey. My prayer is that sharing my soul in these transparent poems will blossom into spiritual blessing for yours and glorify our precious Savior.

When the children of Israel came to Elim in the wilderness, they discovered refreshment by seventy palm trees and twelve wells of water. What a contrast this lush, fertile oasis must have presented to them, against the backdrop of the barren desert!

Experience these seventy reflective poems—like wind-blown palm fronds, gathered and woven into a basket of poetry, for your enjoyment and contemplation!

And they came to Elim, where were twelve wells of water,
and threescore and ten palm trees:
and they encamped there by the waters."
(Exodus 15:27)

PART 1

Supernatural Attributes of God

Riding the Wind in Garments of Light

Oh Lord, how glorious and majestic you are
Your vastness unplumbed through galaxies and bright stars!
The heavens declare your magnificence and might
So stunningly cloaked in dazzling garments of light!

Through the light or the night, your perception shines true
Time and space—constraints both inferior for you
Clouds serve as your chariot soaring through the sky
The wind lifts your wings, omnipresent your sight!

This wonderful world feels the touch of your fingers
Your spirit and quintessence everywhere lingers
Plants and animals in thriving habitations
Fluid symbiosis on land or in oceans.

Both massive or miniscule, all measuring scales
All muscular, powerful or fragile and frail
Your artistic genius deserves our heart's praise
Each season, we're awed by spectacular displays!

Your throne reigns in heaven and earth sits your footstool
Dominions and all kingdoms will bow to your rule
Intricately, attentively designed, each part
Creation's crowning touch we are, sharing your heart!

"Who coverest thyself with light as with a garment...
Who maketh the clouds his chariot
Who walketh upon the wings of the wind"
(Psalms 104:2,3)

Loving Phenomena

Suspend a spinning globe in air
Create eternal souls from dust
Words speak to grow a garden fair
Flip on lights in the void darkness.

The heavens turn like a spigot
To overflow a filthy tub
Angel's food drop on a blanket
Nations control just like puppets.

A deadly weapon from a sling
Commanding secrets from above
A shepherd boy into a king
Who plays his harp with psalms of love.

A virgin births a baby boy
In humble prince's nursery
The man of sorrows imparts joy
Poor beggars healed as royalty.

A mountain level with a seed
Pay Peter's tax from a fish bank
A small lunch stretch, thousands to feed
A hungry little boy to thank.

The liberator bound in chains
The Holy dies a dirty thief
The dead one now in heaven reigns
His doubting church converts, believes.

Miraculous acts from God's Word
Omnipotent power is flexed
Motivated through the ages
By love, the human race to bless!

*"What is the exceeding greatness of his power to us-ward who believe,
according to the working of his mighty power" (Ephesians 1:19)*

God's Three Omni's

Just like ideas and our thoughts
Don't try to stuff God in a box!
He's too expansive to stay there
God's **omnipresent**, everywhere!

God's awesome power stands alone
His muscles flex harder than stone
No load's too heavy for his arm
Omnipotent, almighty, strong!

Sometimes, God can't be figured out
Our minds predict what He's about
Wiser than the best computer
He's **omniscient**, more clever!

Three glories blended perfectly
Never an *"oops!"* eternal, free
In nature, life and Bible see…
This triune God loves little me!

"The heaven of heavens cannot contain thee."
(I Kings 8:27)

PART II

Our Glorious Lord Jesus Christ

This Bottomless Golden Bowl

Unfathomable bowl of gold
Filled with intriguing manna, old
God's bread of life on waters cast
Deity here, on earth at last!

Eternal God, without ending
Love, sweet, divine—kneeling, bending
To us humans, mercy sending
Sacrificing, misery ending.

Pure perfection with glory blessed
Shrouded in humble tent of flesh
Under dull coverings, dingy hues
Hiding the purple, reds and blues.

Manna of life, each morning new
Wafers—"What was it?"—served on dew
Human Jesus weary by well
God incarnate calming the swell.

Atoning great High Priest, for sin
Past veil, with blood, He enters in
Victorious one conquering death
Bursting through tomb with living breath!

Ascended…right hand of God's throne
Intercedes always, when we groan
Returning husband for his bride
Connected by his wounded side.

What was the manna in that bowl?
Who is this Jesus Lord, we know?
All eternity we'll ponder
Exploring God's ceaseless wonder!

…the ark of the covenant…wherein was the
golden pot that had manna" (Hebrews 9:4)

Human Deity

Jesus, precious, innocent, sweet
For meditation such a feast!
Cosmos creator over all
Tucked in a baby's body small.

Hardship birthed, wrapped in a manger
Incarnate God, earthly stranger
Baffling, puzzling to understand
Mighty God and tiny human!

Ruling power, prevailing love
Leaving your royal home above
Rescuing us in our great need
Foreknowing where this road would lead.

Rejection suffering from the start
Agape love poured from your heart
Supernatural healing might
Altruistic for human plight.

Nailed to a cruel cross of wood
And purposely misunderstood
Shedding your sacred, precious blood
Draining God's wrath for our sins' flood.

Task then complete, you left this place
Bequeathing us your love and grace
Displaying up there passion's signs
Human body, nail-scarred, divine.

Returning soon to swoop us there
Immortality with you share
Since you humbled yourself so low
Your glory will forever glow!

*"Christ Jesus, who being in the form of God, thought it not
robbery to be equal with God: But made himself of no
reputation, and…was made in the likeness of men…he humbled himself,
and became obedient unto death, even the death of the cross." (Phillippians 2:5-8)*

Blended Perfection

Mary carried "that holy thing"
God's Son and everlasting King
From heaven to womb, sent so low
Love gift to world, with baby glow!

Jesus—weak infant, manger born
Scandalous setting, full of scorn.
Growing toddler—then stalked to kill
Child—developing boyhood skills.

Jesus—young man, rudely abased
By our evil destitute race
Divine altruistic power
Sin's effects to sense and conquer.

God in Christ, through human stages…
Journey penned in Bible pages
Empathizing, weeping, caring
Our experiences sharing.

Sacrificed on Calvary's tree
Nailed there a slave of love for me.
"Hush!" as this holy gift stripped bare!
So of his riches we could share.

Highly exalted on his throne
With worthy worship He is crowned.
The humbled Christ now glorified
God's love above, personified!

How can our minds rise up with pride?
He wears for us a wounded side.
With grateful hearts, we seek to praise
Him serve and honor all our days.

*"The Word was made flesh, and dwelt among us, (and we beheld his glory,
the glory as of the only begotten of the Father,) full of grace and truth." (John 1:14)*

Answering Questions

Jesus asked so many questions
In his short earthly journey here
Soul-provoking ones, reflections
Listeners' affections to endear.

His questions still ring relevant
A spotlight searching out our souls
Disentangling past and present
Progressive path, escorting home.

"Who do you say I am?" He raised
"A teacher, prophet, just a man?"
Did not his miracles amaze
Fulfill all prophecies as planned?

*"What's it worth for a wealthy heir
If soul is lost and left behind?"*
His soul with wealth can't be compared
Only Jesus can save mankind.

"What is it I can do for you?"
The risen Lord is asking me?
*"Lord, wash my sins, make me anew
Enter my heart, release, set free!"*

*"Why are you worried and you fret?
Do you lack anything, today?"*
From shining sunrise to sunset
More than my needs in wondrous ways.

"Who touched me?" *"Lord, connect with me
I crave more faith, more grace, more song.
It finally dawns, my heart believes
You've been the answer all along!"*

Jesus in the Window

Searching the mysteries in his eyes
Drawing the curtain but a pinch
Two twinkling stars from heaven's skies
Immortal glories, just a hint.

Jesus Christ with human vision
Compassion, empathy and groans
My heart's sorrows to enlighten
His tears to mingle with my own.

Lens penetrating all men's thoughts
Macro, micro, past and future
Calculating plans and subplots
Tactful, hearts and minds to capture.

Red smoking burning coals of fire
Protective of God's dignity
Rotten hypocritical mire
Of Saducees and Pharisees.

Glist'ning diamonds, sparkling glory!
Crystals reflecting purest light!
Unveiled fleeting kingly splendor
Concentering disciples' sight.

Blood-shot, hot tears weeping, swollen
Christ's eyelids closed on Calvary's tree.
On high, unseen eyes beholding
Guiding, smiling, down here on me.

My Lord's eyes, adore and fathom
(Smitten, captivated sweetly)
Someday plumb those volumes, awesome
Understood and loved, uniquely!

Where Is He?

Mary tucked him in the crude hay
on the softest spot she could find.
John held his head 'neath Jordan's wave
foreshadowing the death He'd die.

Satan led him to a wasteland
tempted, He glowed—pure fragrant rose.
Peaceful king, as foretold, preplanned
hoisted on a lowly burro.

Haters nailed to Calvary's cross
surrendered lamb with bleeding feet.
Placed in gloomy tomb with pathos
stopped, deceased, that loving heartbeat.

God raised his Son from dreary tomb
completely satisfied, endeared!
Seated him in heaven's throne room
soon for his bride to reappear.

In our hearts, where have we ranked him?
Does He reign royal king, supreme?
Or outside ling'ring, distant, dim
sadly neglected, not esteemed?

"Behold I stand at the door, and knock:
If any man hear my voice and open the door,
I will come in to him and will sup with him, and He with me."
(Revelation 3:20)

The "Est" of Jesus

The **meekest** Sovereign descended his throne
Renounced its splendor, rich glory and all
For slums and squalor. Such humble love shown!
The ultimate grandest shrank so, so small.

The **gladdest** human who graced this sad earth
Transformed water to wine, cheering friends' days
Diffused the perfume of spiritual mirth
Splashed joyful delight on dingy byways!

The **holiest** Priest cloaked in human skin
Glowed genuine gold in the tempter's fire
Though truly recoiled by the stench of sin
He rescued us from its slimy quagmire.

The **saddest** man, "Jesus wept" with us here
Empathy, sympathy, feeling our pain
Callously crucified with taunts and sneers
The "Man of Sorrows" expired there, tear-stained.

The **most victorious** Conqueror, great
Defeated the devil and death and sin
The Lord of lords, Ruler and Magistrate
Merited praises, forever, we'll sing!

Jesus, superlatives, surpassing one
Actions and words and love beyond compare
Chief over thousands and second to none
Singular object, my soul's solitaire!

"That in all things He might have the preeminence."
(Colossians 1:18)

PART III

Streaming Biblical Themes

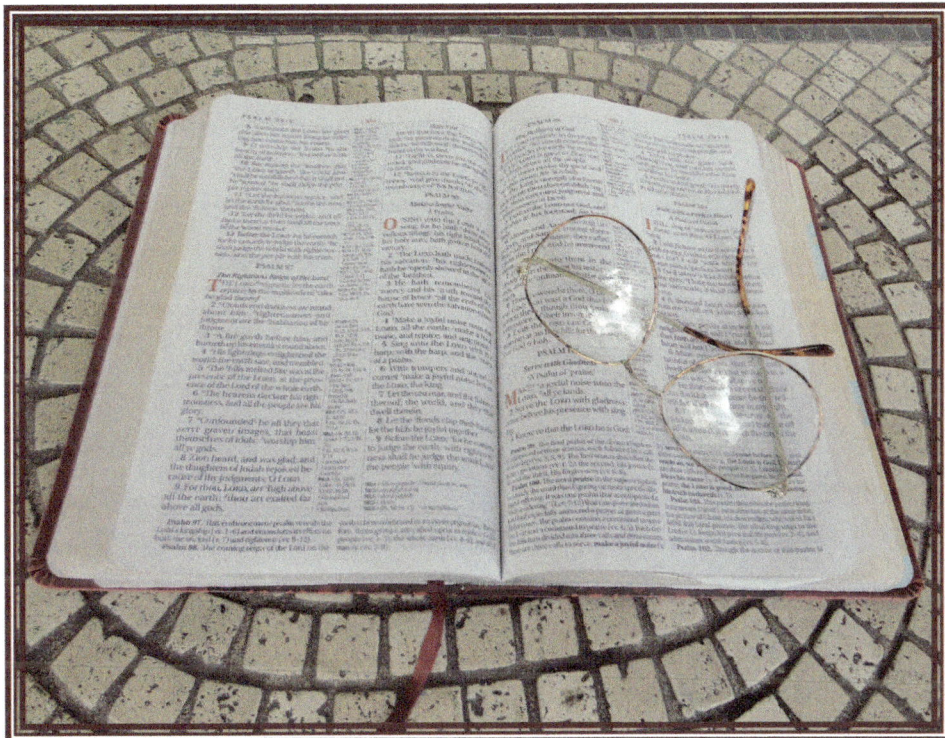

The Read of a Lifetime

The BIBLE beckons…a great adventure
Deserving every person's attention
Well might you ponder, "Why should I bother?"
The Bible breathes from cover to cover!
Sixty-six books by forty chosen men
Yet God spoke inside them, moving their pens
Spanning fifteen hundred years to complete
Not one discrepancy, very discreet!

Presented two: Old and New Testaments
Old scrolls scripted with Jewish perspective
Imagine creation when time began!
Intriguing diaries of women and men
Patriarchs, prophets, poor paupers, rich kings
Sweet psalmist, David penned poems to sing
Wisdom of Proverbs for all of us fools
Solomon's knowledge from heaven's high school.

From verses to chapters to books behold
History…His story being retold
Spotlight on Him, His agenda, not ours
We're humans, not heroes or superstars
Just privileged objects of undeserved love
Jesus descended from heaven above.

Perfectly on-cue, unveiled in the New
Messianic prophecies all came true
Magical miracles orchestrated
In sync with his Father, love translated!
Sacrificed on the cross, Christ sets us free
Devil and death conquered, eternally
Risen, ascended to God's throne above
Devotedly interceding in love!

After the Gospels, the mailman arrives
Apostles' letters for churches to thrive
From lonely islands and prisons, dingy
Emerge precious secrets and mysteries!
Future's unrolled, Revelation's timeline
The Church soon ushered to heaven's shoreline
The devil and wicked heaved into hell
Then, New Jerusalem, gemmed and four-square!

In book form, tablet or app on your cell
In memory and heart, the gospel to tell
The Scriptures impart inspiration sweet
Two-edged sword, evil devil defeat!
They refill our vaults with the love of God
A map and flashlight for this path untrod
Some cool soothing salve for hot, oozing sores
Fluid stream of prose, on-line or in stores!

We're all engrossed in life's crazy rat race
Let's just take ten, nothing else can replace
Meditate daily on God's rich treasure
Tomorrow and today, blessed together!
Then when the pages fade, dog-eared and stained
Son rays have beamed out, the good news campaigned!

"The law of the Lord is perfect, converting the soul:
the testimony of the Lord is sure, making wise the simple…
more to be desired are they than gold, yea, than much fine gold:
sweeter also than honey and the honeycomb." (Psalm 19:7, 10)

Writing with Light and Blotting with Love

On stony tablet, palace wall
Sand, sky and hearts of flesh
God's fingers loudly etch it all
Our souls exposed to bless.

The message impressed by the light
Disgraceful sin reveals
Frantic to scatter after night
Like rats by dark concealed.

His tender heart expresses thoughts
Where light and love are wed
For in the Books of Life, He blots
Out sin with ink that's red!

"The blood of Jesus Christ his son cleanseth us from all sin"
(I John 1:7)

I Am Not but I Have Lots

I am not a super Christian
But I love my superb Savior
One who pitied my position
Died to show me grace and favor.

I am not a super Christian
But possess splendid salvation
Relationship, not religion
Jesus' friendship and compassion.

I am not a super Christian
But respect my heav'nly Father
One who cares for all his children
Dearly loves his sons and daughters!

I am not a super Christian
But inside resides the Spirit
My salvation's seal and earnest
Of the riches I'll inherit.

I am not a super Christian
But part of a huge family
World-wide brothers, lots of sisters
Reveling in diversity!

I am not a super Christian
But expect a blessed future
Mansion with my Lord in heaven
Reserved home, unfading luster!

God's tremendous gifts shine perfect
Showered toward unworthy me
He deserves the praise and worship
Pursuing and preserving me!

"But we all, with open face beholding as in a glass the glory of the Lord, are changed into the same image from glory to glory" (2 Corinthians 3:18)

Crumbling Shutters

I stumbled down a dark hall, windows shuttered tight
But through a crack, a light beam stole revealing that
My awful rotten sinful soul smelled quite a fright!

God could propel me straight to hell, what I deserved
My sins killed Jesus. Sadly that was the reason
He must be sacrificed, lamb for altar reserved.

As I wept, shutters tumbled from the first window
Forgiving grace saved my soul. Christ renewed me whole!
Born again, a tiny babe, prepared now to grow.

But troubling doubts distressed, especially when I sinned
My conscience produced fear. Peace and joy disappeared.
Yet, *"None can pluck from His hand,"* nothing could rescind.

Again sunbeams gleamed—peaceful comprehension!
Holy Spirit dwelling, Jesus Christ revealing
Inspiration stirred and prompted motivation!

But the old nature seemed to triumph over me
Many times defeating, though I tried repeating
Scriptures read, *"Consider it dead,"* for victory!

Someday I'll skip with Jesus, heaven's halls of gold
Darkness dissipating, sparkling light cascading!
As Jesus, further clarity to me unfolds.

*"For God who commanded the light to shine out of darkness
hath shined in our hearts, to give the light of the knowledge
of the glory of God in the face of Jesus Christ." (2 Corinthians 4:6)*

Two Roots and Their Fruit

Jesus conquered both root and fruit
Dying on Calvary for me
Redemptive work…Yes, Hallelu!
Sins washed away, eternally.

Potential death blow to the root
Adam's old nature that still sins.
Instilled a new one, what a beaut!
Never can sin, lives too within.

Master Gardener of my heart
Patiently tends and intercedes
Without his priestly, pruning art
My garden'd be a field of weeds!

Someday, the sin root will drop dead
Right now, I'll nourish the new vine
Flourishing, luscious fruit ahead
Grapes of joy, love and peace, sublime!

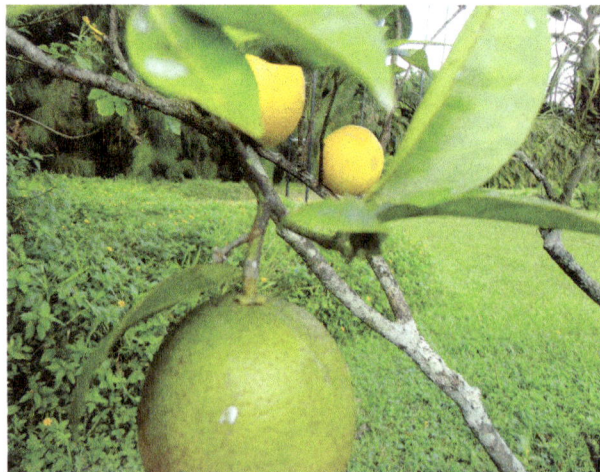

*"But, now being made free from sin, and become
servants to God, ye have your fruit unto holiness,
and the end everlasting life." (Romans 6:21)*

Comparing Paradoxes

Preciousness press out of the vile
From ashes rises new beauty
Rags exchange for royal textiles
Relative or absolutely?

Seemingly strong—really a child
The wise deluded, a duped fool
The last ranks first, though he acts mild
Worldly glory ends miniscule.

Dark night illumines into day
Cold winter thaws to summer fair
Tears glisten, iridescent ray
Calm peace usurps nightmarish scare!

Love loves away the hater's hate
Huge debts are cancelled, not repaid
"Grace stands just," rules the magistrate
The human God, Jesus displayed!

A cruel cross exalted Him
Death circled back to life again
Hellish loss gained heavenly win
The conquered one now reigns, Amen!

*"For my thoughts are not your thoughts,
neither are your ways my ways, saith the Lord.
For as the heavens are higher than the earth,
so are my ways…and thoughts" (Isaiah 55:8,9)*

Welcome Home

At heaven's address, love's banner waves high
Temporal earthly spheres fail to compare
The banquet's prepared, come feast on the sight
Magnificent mansion, Jesus prepared!

Formerly sinners, now saved saints galore
Singing his praises surrounding the throne
Bragging rights disallowed, none keeping score
All saved by simply grace, through faith alone
in the grace room

Hebrews eleven, Old Testament guests
Embracing promises viewed from afar
Credit for simple trust, passing all tests
Loved, earthly friends of the bridegroom, they are
in the faith room

Captives of filthy sins, dirty and rank
Only the Holy One, virtuous, pure
Paid debt in full, took his blood to the bank
Ransomed the prisoners, safe and secure
in the redemption room

Born and adopted, God's blessed children
Heirs of inheritance, a varied clan
Sharing genetic traits, discipline, fun
Pre-destined, before the old world began
in the family room

Baby lambs, feeding on velvet green grass
Disabled, unable, to understand
He sought and carried them, tenderly blessed
Healed of their handicap in this new land
in the shepherd's room

What will the dynamics, dimensions be?
Surely undreamable by you or me
With our very eyes, yes, Jesus we'll see!
The key to our home comes from Calvary!

*"In my Father's house are many mansions…I go to prepare a place for you…
that where I am, there ye may be also." (John 14:2,3)*

The Future Teller

What instigates this world's demise
Abduction from alien guys
Global warming (the icebergs die)
Nuclear explosions in the skies?

Masked, hides the future, undisclosed
But, in the last book of God's Word
Two thousand years, church history flows
Despite long struggles, God's her Lord.

Evil days increase much worse
Jesus snatches away his church
Moral decaying bubble burst
Exclaim, *"good riddance"* to this earth!

Gospel meetings, forsaken, ceased
Deceived lie lovers left behind
They'll still disdain the Prince of Peace
Years, fearful seven, then unwind.

Sweet wedding bells above will chime
Jesus will wed the church, his bride
On earth, the trinity of crime
Beast, the devil and anti-Christ.

Hebrew calendar then resumes
God keeps the promises He made
Jewish remnant rose, in full bloom
She'll claim the nail holes, weep and pray.

Christ on white horse bolts through the sky
All enemies completely crushed
He'll reign a thousand years, sublime
Back to the garden, green and lush!

Satan and sinners…lake of fire
Judge God concludes, *"You go to hell!"*
New heavens, earth, inhale the air
Fair, gemmed Jerusalem, four square!

God's timeline in his Word's revealed
A pathway to salvation bright
Apocalypse, cyclone, disease?
No, much worse plight, eternal night!

PART IV

Just Mundane Fun?

Driven For Him

I totaled my clunker, what disaster!
Traded the wreckage for new Christian life
Captivating, faith-raising adventure
Enjoy the ride with me! Christ paid the price.

Turn key in ignition and *"vroom"* it starts
Initiating sparkplugs and engine
God's love excited, ignited my heart
Started my spiritual engine humming!

Strapping my seat belt's the law, to keep safe
Protect me from harm, bar an accident
Coffee, reading and prayer…day starts with grace
Jewels journey with safety and substance.

Pedal to the metal, away I go!
Energized by the power, God's Spirit
Motivating my soul, fueling my growth
To progress and mature in Christ's precepts.

Brake pedal, must trust. Don't hit anyone!
Red sin signs yell *"Stop!"* or yield pain and tears
Bar the old nature, trouble-maker shun
Bad temptations detour 'round, all my years.

Both hands on the steering wheel, left or right
Directions follow by map, GPS
The Spirit of God directs me aright
Searching Bible for guidelines, not guesses.

Tires require inflation enough
Always discouragement deflates my soul
Thick tread for rough roads, built hardy and tough
Needed courage for deep muddy pot-holes.

Back and forth, back and forth, the wipers *"whoosh"*
Pounding rain, on windshield, blurring focus
Storms seem to wash with tears, clear and unloose
Distracting trivial, leaving purpose.

How could I drive without headlights at night?
I like wider brights that broaden my scope
The Bible shines like a streaming streetlight
Misty gloom piercing with glimmering hope!

Motoring on by my Savior sustained
Singing God's praises, passengers along
Denying distractions, destiny gained
In heaven with Jesus, where I belong!

"Bon Appetit" at the Bible Diner

Abraham and Sarah baked guests a feast
of freshly baked cakes and tender, young beef.
Esau, twin brother, smelled Jacob's good stew
bought with his birthright, not loved nor valued.

Brothers of Joseph, the famine trimmed thin
feasting in Egypt, he sure surprised them!

Israelites roasted the Passover lamb
shoes on their feet and a staff in their hand.
Manna, honey wafers, served on wet dew
for forty long years, would you complain too?

Morning and evening, Elijah would look
for meals on wings, ravens served by the brook!

Mephibosheth ate at the king's table
safe handicapped place for this disabled.
Royally, Esther planned with protocol
preventing her people's genocide fall!

The Lord was invited to Matthew's meal
with sin sickly publicans, He could heal.

Fussing and fretting, tired Martha worked hard
service though, she learned should spring from the heart!
With Jesus, a small lad just shared his snack
five thousand people ate and no one lacked!

Jesus loved the last supper with dear friends
we, too remember—his death comprehend.

Hungry disciples smelled hot sizzling fish
their risen Lord frying a breakfast dish!
Our gracious girded host, Jesus the Lord
will nourish and serve us, forevermore!

The Winner's Strategies

Our God, skilled puzzle-maker
connecting shapes together
the people mover, shaker
communities forever

Rich Boardwalk, matching Park Place
comptroller, heaven's banker
"get out of jail", sins erased
our soul's financial planner

Thee genius chess player
shuffling royal kings and queens
political pawn maker
behind all scenes, though not seen

Scheming video gamer
fighting terroristic wars
'till God, the violence tamer
reigns in peace, forevermore

Salvation stays his end game
strategizing to win hearts
riches, wisdom, power aim
to defeat the devil's game!

*"All things work together for good
to them that love God, to them that
are the called according to his purpose"*
(Romans 8:28)

The Football of Faith

Quarterback to wide-receiver
Soaring over crashing helmets
Deafening roar from fan cheer-leaders!
Solid catch! Can you believe it?

Starting, darting through the mazes
Mates protecting him from tackle
Speed he needs as on he races
Reaching goal-line looms the battle!

When God throws you the ball of faith
Snatch it! Hug it! Protect with life!
If you fumble, quickly retake
The Christian life is worth the fight.

Dragged down by trials and by sin
Diasters knocking out your feet
Targeted from without, within
With God your coach, go beat defeat!

Yea! Jesus fans and Christian friends
Give all and leave all, when you fight
Hold tight to faith and at game's end
Your testimony—Dynamite!

"Fight the good fight of faith" (I Timothy 6:12)

Hula-Hooping Rings

Swirling, hula, twirling, hooping
circumstances doing dances
in then out around the looping
God or incidental chances?

Family tree, a born-in ring
dangling, jangling, glistening cheers
or swinging from it, spider strings
community with laughs and tears!

Nine long months a growing tenant
looping tight cords around mom's heart
now encircled, endless parent
age or stage…always her sweetheart!

Ring extends, the child leans, reaching
siblings and pals, friends and puppies
learning lessons, others teaching
tons of fun and sometimes muddy!

The sparkly ring, a diamond thing
promises flashing, wedding day
flowing gown, the trail a-twirling
marriage gift-wrapped in a bouquet.

Olympic rings, heated, burning
competition smoke dust blowing
peace talks keep the table turning
tension, turbulence swirls…growing.

Relational parts overlap
reciprocation starts and stops
cell phones ringing, *"I'll call asap!"*
communication, keep or drop.

Our culture serenades of love
broken hearts and dreams and longings
but praises for God's love above
rings eternal and belonging!

"…fitly joined together…" (Ephesians 4:16)

Poetic Potpourri

I ponder...shall I ever know
A tree ugly as Calvary
Where Jesus moaned and groaned for me
There suffering untold agony?

When a sinner weeps over sin
Bows his head and prays
I perceive the Spirit like wind
Moving in to stay.

There are two paths and we must choose
Which one to take. They intersect
The most liked, wanders wide and loose
The narrow one maintains the truth.
On one you're blessed, the other wrecked!

There really is no question, Hamlet
'Cause, life's a shining precious treasure
Its author, Prince of Life, the donor
Decides the mixture, moods and measure.

INDEED YOUR LONG PLAYS HAVE BEEN STAGED
THE WHOLE WORLD TO AMAZE
BUT, JESUS ALSO GRACED THIS STAGE
HIS LAST DISPENSATIONS!

This life is fleeting, but it's real
Dreams also feel serenely real
Life gets jumbled and gets bumbled
And sand castles, well they crumble
Not brevity devalues worth
With Christ's eternal life, on earth.

Tuck Jesus in your soul
the scriptures in your mind
They'll cheer, hug and console
you...each and every time!

Reflections on:
1. "Trees" by Joyce Kilmer 2. "Who Has Seen the Wind" by Christina Rosetti 3. "The Road Not Taken" by Robert Frost 4. "To Be or Not To Be" and "All the World's a Stage" by William Shakespeare 5. "A Dream within a Dream" by Edgar Allen Poe 6. "Keep a Poem in Your Pocket" by Beatrice Shenk de Regniers

Chasing Insomnia with Jesus

Last night I flopped in bed real late
so drained, exhausted, I couldn't wait.
On the pillow, I plunked my head
but, then my mind woke up instead!

Occasions of the day replayed
actions, words and feelings surveyed.
To the future then I hurried
studied, tarried and I worried.

Interceding, to God pleading
family and all God's people.
They were probably fast asleep
while I, a night watch had to keep!

The hours slowly dawdled on
then, fading darkness hinted dawn.

Pillow of Jacob, solid stone
dreamy ladder up to God's throne
the angels floated up and down
how captivating and spellbound!

Job and David both shared my plight
God sent them love songs in the night.

And even though I turned and tossed
sleep needed, really wasn't lost
my joy, exquisite company
'cause Jesus spent the night with me!

"He giveth his beloved sleep" (Psalm 127:2)

Human Anatomy & Physiology 101

We are fearfully, wonderfully made
God's crowning creation, of the sixth day
Designed intelligence, his praise displays
Reflecting his image all of our days.

Systems of organs, of tissues, of cells
Involuntary reflex, we can't tell
We're in control of voluntary ones
Active life-styles, living healthy as well.

Circulatory starts, four-chambered heart
Oxygenated blood flows to all parts
Heart is the engine on which we rely
Without endless pumping, we would all die.

Respiratory, we need healthy lungs
Where oxygen for our body comes from
Inhale the fresh air, oxygen receive
Exhale, release, carbon dioxide leaves.

The nervous system begins at the brain
Perceptive computer, starting the maze
Relaying-pleasure nerves or the *"ouch"* pain
Through spinal cord back, then to brain again.

Integumentary…nail, skin and hair
Without them, we'd be (oh, no!) bald and bare!
Security system guarding outside
"Not on my watch!" this clean germaphobe cries.

More muscles, ligaments, tendons galore!
Attaching, supporting, all of the bones
Joints, chords and pulleys working together
Exercise makes the skeletal better.

Our rumbly tummy growls, *"I'm hungry, please*
Breakfast, lunch and dinner—three healthy meals!"
Digestion starts when you put food in mouth
Moves to the stomach, intestines, then south.

In urinary…*flush!* The water works
"Where is the bathroom? My full bladder hurts!"
Kidney pipes filter the blood so it's pure
Don't dehydrate, drink water, then drink more!

Immune antibodies help keep us well
A fierce battle rages within our cells
White cells and lymph glands form strong defenses
On the front lines, *"Disease, no advances!"*

Awesome miracle, how we all started!
Parent genes met and amalgamated.
Children, most precious, from God in heaven
Lovingly gifted to men and women.

Our engineered, human body, complex
All impressive systems interconnect
The medical field might never retrieve
All of its mysteries left to unweave.

Genius, our creative designer
Second time 'round, we'll be even better
Remodeled new in immortal fashion
Superbly suited, like Him, for heaven!

"I will praise thee, for I am fearfully and wonderfully made."
(Psalm 139:14)

Predictions from David's Sundial

THIS BRIDEGROOM SPRINTS ACROSS THE SKY
HE'S CHASING HIS GOOD-HUMORED BRIDE
HER STARRY EYES AND MOONY GRIN
ELUDE HIM NIGHTLY WITH CHAGRIN!

TICK-TOCKERS BURIED DEEP IN CHESTS
AN HOUR GLASS IN CLAY JAR SET
IF BLOOD CLOTS BLOCK THIS THUMPING CLOCK
MY SOUL WILL SOAR TO HEAVEN'S DOCK!

ANOTHER GROOM LONGS FOR HIS BRIDE
YEARNS FOR HER BEAUTY BY HIS SIDE
HER EYES TOO SHINE THROUGH THIS WORLD'S NIGHT
NOT HIDING, CRAVING, FOR HIS LIGHT!

"THE SUN, WHICH IS AS A BRIDEGROOM,
COMING OUT OF HIS CHAMBER,
AND REJOICETH AS A STRONG MAN TO RUN A RACE.
HIS GOING FORTH IS FROM THE END OF HEAVEN,
AND HIS CIRCUIT UNTO THE ENDS OF IT"
(PSALM 19:4-6)

PART V

Bible Adventures and Surprises for Kids

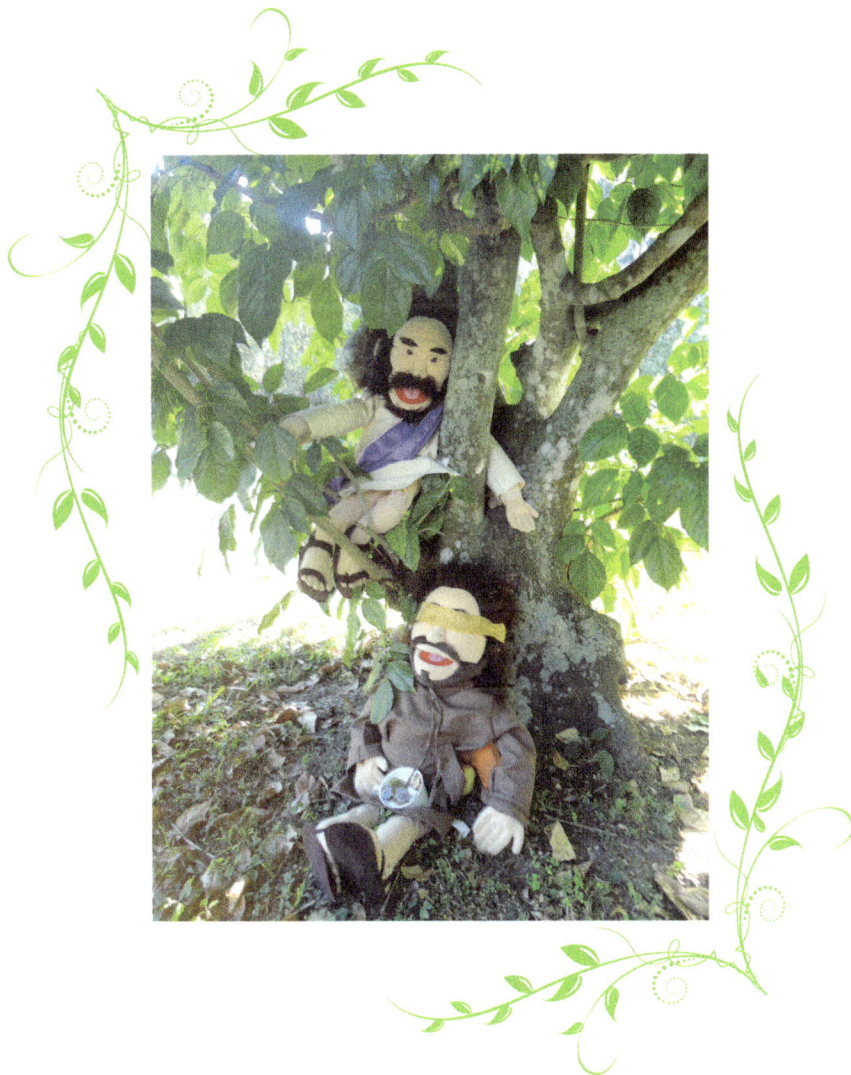

Joy from a Little Boy

Today the angels had more joy
More joy because a little boy
Heard the happy gospel story
Jesus came to earth from glory.

And died upon a cruel tree
So that from sin he could be free.
He heard that Jesus' blood was shed
To wash away his sins, so bad.

He simply bowed his little head
And in his quiet heart, he said,
*"Dear Jesus, I have been quite bad
I know that it has made you sad.*

*I am sorry! I can see
That you died on the cross for me.
Please come into my heart right now
Yes, save me! Only you know how!"*

The Savior heard him loud and clear
And knew that he had been sincere
His heart of love stretched from heaven
Saved this precious boy, age seven!

This little boy was born again
Heaven-ready, a new Christian
Preserved from hell. It was so real
His sweet grin reached from ear to ear!

If you're not saved, please do this, do!
Jesus also died for you, too.
He loves you more, you'll never know!
Believing in Him saves your soul.

In heaven there will be more joy
Resulting from a girl or boy
Who simply took God at his word
Confessed, *"Yes, Jesus is my Lord!"*

*"There is joy in the presence of the angels
of God over one sinner that repenteth." (Luke 15:10)*

Dipping our Toe in the Ocean

Imagination of God's earth
appreciate creation's worth.
So many colors, blends and hues
fuchsia, magenta, aqua blue.

What about the human races?
Let's admire all their faces
black and white, such variation
what a wonderful creation!
hair that's black and curly, kinky
hair that's blond and straight and slinky.

Picture all the animals too
Remember the ones from the zoo?
skinny giraffes with stretchy necks
huge elephants, fleas small as specks
zebras with stripes, leopards' pop spots
monstrous and dainty, streaks and dots
funny monkeys swinging in trees
terrifying lions, quick, freeze!

This experience used your eyes
but what about smells, tastes and cries?
In the garden you smelled a rose
scented fragrance tickled your nose!
Fanciful flavors, they don't stop
like yummy ones in ice-cream shops.

The kitten's soft with silky fur
when you caress it, it hums, *"purrrr"*

Stop! Stop! Don't touch a porcupine
his warning sticks, a prickly spine!
Hear the canary sing, *"tweet, tweet!"*
no human voice can sound so sweet.

God so awesomely made our world
Dip your toe in the ocean and
swirl, swirl, swirl!

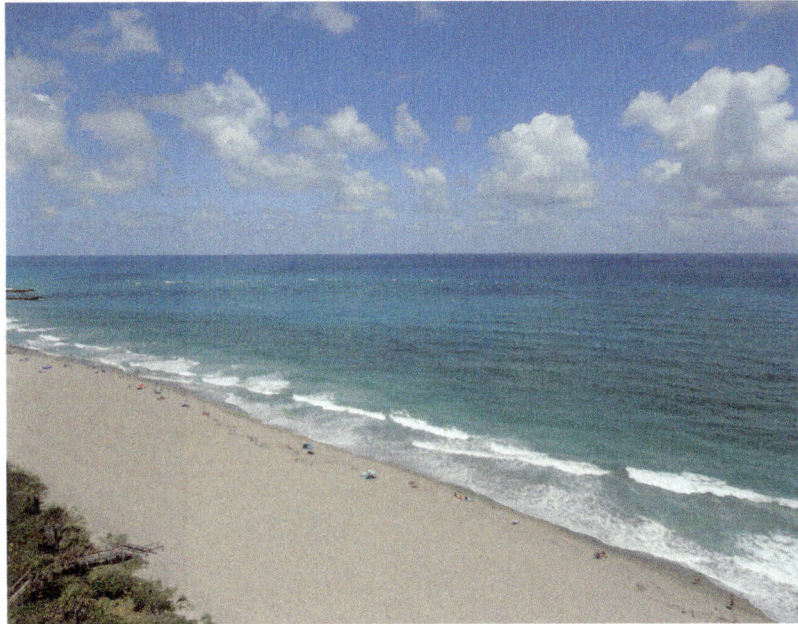

"O Lord, how manifold are thy works! In wisdom hast thou made them all the earth is full of thy riches." (Psalm 104:24)

Mr. Rich and Lazarus Poor

Two men lived who knew each other
One was rich, other a beggar.
Mr. Rich wore clothes of purple
Mr. Poor, torn rags, quite awful.

The wealthy one enjoyed good food
The hungry beggar on crumbs chewed.
Many partied with Mr. Rich
The beggar's friends, dogs from a ditch.

Mr. Rich felt healthy and strong
Mr. Poor felt sickly, prolonged
Without warning, both lives ended
Do you know where their souls landed?

Lazarus Poor to heaven went
Because he was poor? No, God sent
His son Jesus to die for sins
His shed blood washes us within.

Mr. Rich, I'm sorry to tell
His money could not save from hell.
Sadly here, he did not believe
Stuck now forever! He can't leave.

But, you and I, are free to choose
Accept Jesus as Lord, or lose.
Can you not hear his loving voice?
Hell is an endless, sad, sad choice!

"The beggar died, and was carried by the angels
into Abraham's bosom: the rich man also died…
And in hell he lift up his eyes, being in torments".
(Luke 16:22, 23)

A-Z Fun with Bible Names

Adam created was never a child
Balaam's donkey talked words, wasn't that wild?
Cain killed his brother, but wasn't sorry
David loved God, a king for his glory

Elijah didn't die, God's prophet of fire
Felix heard Paul preach, but was not inspired
Goliath monster, was killed by a stone
Hannah gave Samuel, coats she had sewn

Isaac on altar, just Abraham's test
Jesus our Savior, forever the best!
Korah, too greedy, died in a sink hole
Luke shows humanity of Jesus' soul

Mary birthed Jesus, in stable with ewes
Noah's ark rode the flood, some noisy zoo!
Othniel, the soldier, won lands and a wife
Paul, the apostle said, *"Christ is my life!"*

Queen of Sheba, picked King Solomon's brains
Ruth moved with Naomi, to gather grains
Solomon's kingdom reigned, rich and far-flung
Timothy, Paul coached, example to young

Uriah, one of David's best soldiers
Vashti replaced by Esther, more noble
Weeping Jeremiah, prophet who cried
Xodus of slaves, had Moses, as guide

Yahweh, Messiah of Jewish people
Zechariah cried: *"Repentance...needful!"*
God knows your name, He's writing your story
Is it God or you gaining the glory?

Fun fact: Some of the Psalms, originally written in the Hebrew, were acrostics.
Psalm 119 contains 8 verses each, for all of the 22 letters in the Hebrew alphabet.

100-1+1

10-1+1

2-1+1

Students, do you take math in school
Addition and subtraction rules?
I have some math for you today
It can be fun, it's more like play!
A story, Jesus told in parts
It really shows His loving heart
He said three things once were missing
(I hope you are really listening!)

The Shepherd had one hundred sheep
But one lamb, Wooly, wouldn't keep…*("baa")*
He jumped the fence and ran away
I think he almost died that day
The shepherd left the ninety-nine
Knew in the fold that they'd be fine
But lost Wooly who went astray?
The shepherd saved his life that day.

Next, this part…a lady had ten
Coins she was saving, up 'till then
Now, only nine. Her heart it sank!
"I should have put them in the bank."
She took a broom and swept her floor
Swish and swish, *(cough!)* *"I should do this more!"*
She, then found it, where I don't know
Stuck in a crack, behind the door?

This story, it has one more part
The son who broke his father's heart
"Dad, this sad dump is no more fun!"
Call him Tom, the prodigal one
At first the father had two sons
With Tom gone, he only had one
His father prayed for Tom, for him
That he'd give up his life of sin.

Tom had friends, till he was flat broke
Hungry, homeless, life was no joke!
Dirty pigs grunted, *"You've been bad"*
So home Tom trudged, shameful and sad
But sadness soon was changed to joy!
The father welcomed home his boy.

This story, thrice shows us clearly
God loves everyone so dearly
He cares for every single one
Not just a few, not just for some
The sum of all things lost was none
God's good at finding everyone!

(Read this story in Luke Chapter 15)

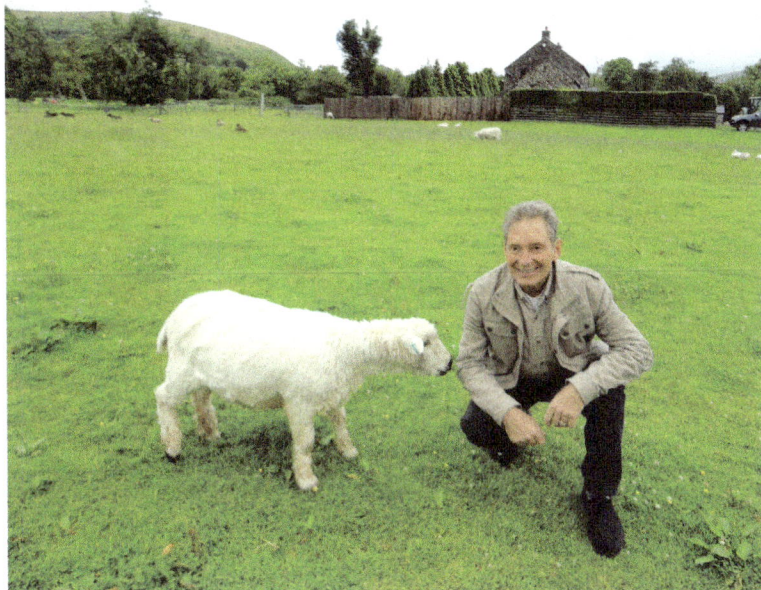

Up from a Pothole and Down a Sycamore Tree

Bartimaeus was blind, his eyes couldn't see
Zacchaeus was short so, he climbed a tree

Zacchaeus was rich, Bartimaeus, poor
Did Jesus feel love for the rich one more?
No never, not Jesus! He cared the same
He knew all about them, even their names

Bart like a coiled spring, *(boing!)*, popped off the ground!
Zac like a squirrel, from tree scampered down!

Zac, the tax man, proved quite hospitable
Beggar Bart, sadly, lived despicable!
They all had a wonderful time that day
But Jesus in Jericho, just couldn't stay

He had a mission, the crowd could not see
He had to be nailed, up Calvary's tree

For us to throw off our dirty rags too
Live with Jesus above, in the sky blue
We'll meet Bartimaeus and Zac, up there
I'm sure they'll have more great stories to tell!

(Read the story about Bartimaeus in Mark 10: 46-52)
(Read the story about Zacchaeus in Luke 19: 1-10)

Not Just "Hee-haw"

Have you ever said something really dumb
And wished instead that you'd bitten your tongue?
Here God prevented it for a reason…
"Don't curse my people, to please the heathen!"

This Bible story's on—Balaam's his name
His little donkey, not him, deserves fame
By Moab's king hired, God's people to curse
This man loved money, some more for his purse.

This cursing acted like casting a spell
Which God, by the way, can easily quell
He asked the Lord, *"Do you want me to go?"*
Whose kidding who? He was joking, this bloke!

He hopped on his donkey and off they rode
An angel soon stopped them, holding a sword
The donkey saw him and started to balk *(hee-haw!)*
When Balaam beat him, this hurt donkey talked! (real words!)

Balaam, distracted about the money
Didn't think talking donkeys were funny
The angel though angry from the abuse
Alerted Balaam of bigger issues.

By King Balak hired, to curse God's people
This sounds like a job that's pretty simple
But every time Balaam opened his mouth
Instead of curses, new blessings came out!

If talking animals, God can create
A puppet too, from a prophet who's fake
The Lord is list'ning to all words we say
Let's try to please him, with our talk today!

(Read this funny story in Numbers 22, 23)

Slimy Fish Guts

Amusement spots, kids can swim with dolphins
But, in this story, the man was swallowed
Inside the big fish, its yucky tummy
This Bible story is kind of funny!

God spoke, *"Jonah, preach to the Ninevites"*
"They're wicked enemies, they have no right!"
Jonah, no, didn't like those folks at all
He tried to run away, ignore the call.

He paid to sail in the opposite way
So God sent a storm and the sailors prayed
They figured out Jonah was the reason
Overboard threw him, feeling uneasy.

God, next, far ahead, prepared a big fish
Who gobbled Jonah up, puny, snack dish
Game playing over, no more hide and seek
Acids attacking made Jonah feel bleak!

Down in a dark dungeon, really slimy!
Slithery, stinky and very grimy
He pleaded with God for another turn
"So sorry, please God," his lesson he'd learned.

This sickish fish felt a big tummy ache!
Ah…eating Jonah had been a mistake
He vomited Jonah, up on the shore
To do the same mission, he had before.

This time, reluctantly Jonah obeyed
This time he did not try, to run away
But, BIG SURPRISE! The people reacted
In Nineveh, repentance erupted!

Slow Jonah learned in the school of a fish
God plans in advance, He's not hit or miss
You can't succeed, don't try running from God
He's too big and loving and weak, He's not!

If you don't believe, He'll go to great lengths
To give you this truth, *"You need to repent."*
Jesus loves folks, even those we dislike
Jonah was fish bait, a nightmarish fright!

Two Camouflaged Lizards

I saw this lizard by the pool
He had been to camouflage school!
He changed the color of his skin
To the envir'nment he was in.

Kids feeling pressured by their peers
Sometimes, conform because of fears
But, this just is another test
You need not be like all the rest.

I found another one inside
He was camouflaged, but he died
Good choices prove most constructive
Bad ones sometimes—quite destructive!

God made no one else just like you!
So honor Him in all you do
Show your colors, always be strong
Follow the Lord, you won't go wrong!

"Let no man despise thy youth;
but be thou an example of the believers,
in word, in conversation, in charity, in spirit,
in faith, in purity. (I Timothy 4:12)

Climbing the Stairs

Prayer's like a floating stair to climb
Past sunny, fluffy clouds sublime
Past planets, galaxies I soar
Faster than lightning, oh much more!

Right to the throne room of the King
My thanks, praise and petitions bring
Then down the ladder, I hope, slides
Angels, laden with surprises!

God's answer might be, *"Patience, child!"*
"Yes!" or *"Are you out of your mind?"*
But always it is wrapped with love
From my wise Father, God above.

So every morning, every night
Before I switch the bedroom lights
I'll climb the stairs where God awaits
To hug me and communicate!

"And he (Jacob) dreamed and behold a ladder set up on the earth, and the top of it reached to heaven: and behold the angels of God ascending and descending on it." (Genesis 28:12)

No Prayer Allowed!

Braver than lions, lived prophet Daniel
Fearless of both, people and animals!
He was commanded, *"No, you must not pray"*
Loving God more, he still prayed each day.

Three times daily, he connected with God
Through open window, his enemies saw
Horribly jealous of his great esteem
Devising this trick with wicked sad scheme.

They conned King Darius to make a law
Staunchly, Daniel did not, his prayers withdraw
Cruelly, in the dungeon they threw him
Those starving lions, they weren't just purring!

Imagine hearing those starved lions, *"ROARR!"*
Like frightful, gigantic tyrannosaurs!
God then sent Daniel a wonderful friend
Down to his den, an angel descended.

Angels are stronger, even than lions
He soon stopped all their loud fuss and crying
Daniel spent an awesome, heaven-like night
In that dark dingy pit with angel bright!

They may have told you too, *"No, you can't pray!"*
Attending secular schools, today
No one controls silent prayer in your heart
Strong faith, just like Daniel's, God can impart.

Just as sure as teachers give tests in school
"Lord, help me with this test" will overrule!
Before you know it, school lessons will end
Eternity soon with Jesus we'll spend.

Anticipate seeing our friend Daniel
Unafraid of both, man or animal
He'll retell the story about that night
Ravenous lions stopped, by angel bright!

(Read this exciting story in Daniel Chapter 6)

*"Praise him with the sound of the trumpet…
the psaltery and harp…the timbrel and dance…
with stringed instruments and organs… upon the loud cymbals…
Let everything that hath breath praise the Lord. (Psalm 150:3-6)*

To the Chief Musician

My orchestra is tuned for praise
The music swells and swirls
All sections interact and surge
God's glory to proclaim.

"Lub-dub-lub-dub" on thumps my drum
Tempo of God's rhythm
Beating, beating: "My God's awesome!"
Onward, marching, onward.

My harp is stringed, heavenly hymns
A fall that drops her shrills
A flowing brook of twangs and trills
Up over worship brims!

"Tee-tootle-tee," flute, *"tootle-tee"*
Sad or squeaking pitches
Cheeping, chirping, whistling chickies
Girls, frilly silly, these.

"Oompah, oompah" brass…ah, blast, ah!
Thundering, booming, strong
Majestically God's band moves on
Trombone, trumpet, tuba.

"Ting, ping, ting, bling…bling, gong, bong, gong!
Percussion zips and zaps
Ecstatically joy pops and claps
My symphony life-long!

VROOOM! ...We're Out of Here!

1. Jesus is coming back again!
    Read it in Thessalonians
    Kind of like we're being captured
    Also Christians call the rapture.

2. Faster than any eye can blink
    Faster than anyone can think
    Vrooom! It's just like a jet-pack
    Securely strapped upon our back!

3. First we are here and then we're there
    High on a cloud up in the air!
    We will see our glorious Lord
    Who, we, on earth, by faith adored.

4. Christians who died before will wake
    From coffins make a prison break
    Together, we will soar above
    To many mansions of God's love!

7. Soon this sad world we'll leave behind
   Eternal joy with Jesus find
   Vrooom! We'll soon be out of here!
   But, are you coming with us, dear?

6. Time is *tick-tick*, ticking away
   Accept Him in your heart today
   There's not lots of time for choosing
   Wait too long, then you'll be losing.

5. I hope that you aren't left behind
   A dreadful nightmare, the real kind
   The Lord died on the cross for you
   To wash your sins and make you new.

"For the Lord himself shall descend from heaven with a shout…
and the dead in Christ shall rise first: Then we which are
alive and remain shall be caught up together with them in
the clouds, to meet the Lord in the air: and so shall we ever
be with the Lord". (I Thessalonians 4:16, 17)

PART VI

Feminine Reflections

The Drawing Room

Poised, yes—pretty, comely, lovely
As bouquet on piano grand
Exquisite in her majesty
She gestures to her guests, who stand
Outside, waiting their acceptance
To her elegant quintessence.

She beckons, *"just one step closer"*
Inch by inch, only as bidden
Such an honor! No one's nobler
Proper protocol in fashion.

God reigns supreme, the King of Kings
Highest, noblest potentate, who
Sacrificed his son for earthlings
Jesus, who died for me and you.
"Draw closer, closer, child, come
Adopted daughters and my sons.

No boundaries, restrictions, lines
Too near to me you cannot be
You flood my heart with joy sublime
For we are royal family!"

"who is the blessed and only Potentate,
the King of kings and Lord of lords…
to whom be honour and power everlasting"
(I Timothy 6:15,16)

Filomene

Cockroaches crawled up the walls of her place
Bedbugs invaded and itched her at night
Husband abused her & slapped, smacked her face
Kidnapped her daughter and life, from her sight.

The surgeon said, *"Sorry, tumor's stage four"*
Chemo crashed in, nauseating and rough
She held her head high and huge burdens bore
The Lord Jesus loved her—that was enough!

Still her strong faith glowed majestically grand
God's glory honored through temporal gray
Jesus spoke softly, *"Dear love, take my hand
Time to go home for…Graduation Day!"*

*"Our light affliction which is but for a moment,
worketh for us a far more exceeding and
eternal weight of glory" (2 Corinthians 4:17)*

"Thus saith the Lord, Set thine house in order"
(2 Kings 20:1)

Spring Cleaning Itch

Springtime brings the housecleaning itch
But, what to keep and what to pitch?
Cluttered pantry of expired goods
Discard "she saids" with old "should'ves"

Restock those shelves with cans of hope
Not botulism poison, nope!
Faith, joy and courage, stack 'em high
In sorrow's hour, off shelf they fly!

In fridge, clean out the frozen mold
Abuse of power chills to cold
Bribing diamonds, not this gal's friend
Jesus—agape to the end.

When oven baked meal tastes like smoke
Crusty pride makes, *"cough"*, others choke!
Humbly scrub, beauty for ashes
Gratitude for gracious blessings.

Who's mopping up that filthy floor?
Good morals just marched out the door
God says it's right—it can't be wrong
Who cares what trends in culture's norm?

Winter clouded up the windows
But, listen now, I hear sparrows…
Jesus returns, *"clean up!"* they sing
Flowers of righteousness He brings!

Uniquely Female

God created females from Adam's rib
We compliment men, love all and rock cribs
What an enchanting, stunning creation!
So closely loved, He brought us salvation.

Exquisite Eve glowed, our clothe she began!
Imagine her olive, blemish-free tan
Flowing long hair and inquisitive eyes
Sadly she fell for the devil's disguise.

Forever childless, made Sarah afraid
Foolishly she lent Abraham, her maid
But in old age, she gave birth to a son
Miraculous promises just begun!

Rachel looked gorgeous. Plain Leah was not
Both Jacob married, by their father's plot
"I'll make you more babies, Jacob love me!
My sister, Rachel is barren, not me."

Ingenius Jochabed, Moses' mom
Infanticide, awful slaughter begun
Probably shaking but praying and brave
Tucked baby in basket. He freed the slaves.

Brave Jael let Sisera enter her tent
"Here sip a glass of milk!" When he was spent
Sound asleep, she took hammer with tent nail
Killed wicked Captain—conquering female!

Ruth, Moabite widow, reaper of crops
Sweet handfuls on purpose, for her were dropped
Faith to Jehovah, then rewarded swell
Kings in her lineage, Jesus, as well.

Princess Tamar, the king's stunning daughter
Sadly, justice, to her was not offered
God told her story, tenderly warns us
Some men are vile and cannot be trusted.

Esther, young Jewess, won beauty contest
Faith and her bravery destined for the test
"For a time such as this," stopped genocide
God, through that nightmare, aligned by her side.

Sweetest, meek Mary submitted to bear
Reproach, undeserved, for honor to share
The Messiah with us, Jesus, her babe
In hay and later, on cross to be laid.

Dear Martha, busy with all the cooking
While sister, Mary, listening and looking
Jesus loved both, Mary chose the best part
Service, my sisters, should spring from the heart!

Joanna, Susanna refreshing Christ
Journeying onward to suffering night
Three Marys crying on Calvary's hill
Saw his dead body there, motionless, still.

Dorcas, the seamstress of garments and coats
Kindness with talent were also of note
When she passed away, she left quite a void
Revived by Peter, again served her Lord.

Stories of maidens, warriors and queens
Low class and high class and all in between
Wonderful women, each with unique tale
Special gems, God loved, distinctly female.

We shine God's women of this present day
Daughters of heaven's king, to whom we pray
With relevant issues of time and place
Situations addressed with poise and grace.

Nourishing families for our loved Lord
Upholding principles found in his Word
Gracefully always, adorn God's glory
Tied with a pink bow, our earthly story!

Gotta Luv Em!

My darling child, do you realize?
For no one else in the whole world
The pain pangs, birth, oh, such surprise!
Proudly announcing flags unfurled.

Tripping toddler, spilling messes
Sleepy eyes and crying matters
Spewing vomit, doctor visits
"Mommy, mommy," chitter chatter.

Unfair coaches, bullies—got friends?
Turning temp up, hot to hotter
Full-time taxi, time and miles end
"You're the best—baseball and soccer!"

B-day candles…older, older
Already romance in the air?
"Careful, keep car off the shoulder!"
Youth groups, Bible study and prayer.

Money tree in yard's been stripped bare
Tuition, rent, computer, books
Our retirement was there, where?
"Study, study—degrees take work!"

Subconsciously in prayers and dreams
I whine and brag so much of you
Listen, right here, right now, my dear
What can I do, do just for you?

"A (mother) cherisheth her children" (I Thessalonians 2:7)

Two Irenes

Together we share the same name, Irene
With God for our king, we're BOTH royal queens.

Skin with genetics—BOTH black and white find
Rich diversity, God's not color-blind!

Tambuka you speak and I use English
Linguistics for BOTH—kinda Christian-ish.

You live in a hut, my roof shingle's blue
BOTH in same mansion, when this life is through.

I cook in my kitchen, you over fire
"Just tasty angel dust" we BOTH desire.

Your kids eat maize, mine American meals
To BOTH as we cook, God whispers, *"Irene!"*

I turn the faucet, you pump yours instead (whew!)
BOTH drink living water, when Scripture's read.

You hand wash clothes, I use washer, dryer
God refreshes BOTH when hot and dog tired!

My car's Suburban; you stroll dusty roads
BOTH ask, *"Lord, which way?"* stopped at a crossroad.

Sadly, you hunger; my war's computers
BOTH reliant on God, absolutely!

You live in Malawi; I'm from the States
Sisters united, BOTH at heaven's gate!

"Now in Christ Jesus…who hath made both one,
and hath broken down the middle wall of partition between us"
(Ephesians 2: 13, 14)

Altogether Lovely

Jesus, romantic gentleman
"My darling love, my sweetest queen"
Opening doors only He can
Opportunities intervened.

If life crowds out our morning date
I sense how much He misses me
"You failed to read my letter, wait…
So many minutes, none for me?"

"Guide me, should I do this or that?
Lord, please precede my kids today"
I cherish our routine chitchat
My confidante and my mainstay.

"No, that is not my point of view
You will understand tomorrow"
Patiently without an argue
He waits for my brain to follow.

"Protecting me with your strong arm
Pulling the bullets from midair
Safely secure and far from harm
Peace fills my heart most everywhere!"

"Your mood, my dear seems gloomy blue
Look, here's a beautiful bouquet
A hearty hug's long overdue
Sweetheart, encouraged be, today!"

"You own the gown and I, the ring
Our mansion? Progress everyday
Perhaps today this song I'll sing
Arise my love and come away!"

"I am my beloved's and my beloved is mine" (Song of Solomon 6:3)

Midlife Surprises

Crinkly wrinkles lurk round my face
Blest symbols of enduring grace
I'm present still, flashing a smile
So stretch those wrinkles into miles!

You have noticed my new color?
Highlights mixed with one another
Same shade for fifty years? …Boring!
Free are these and hair's my glory.

Where did my skinny figure go?
Same appetite, but now I grow
Extra layers, curves and more weight
Thank God for bounty on my plate!

Sometimes, I think I live with thieves
Many things keep disappearing
I've scattered there a dozen pair
In house and car and everywhere.

This slowing down, decreasing strength
Is dwindling less the journey's length
Supplies will last. I'm in God's care
Forever young, I'll thrive up there!

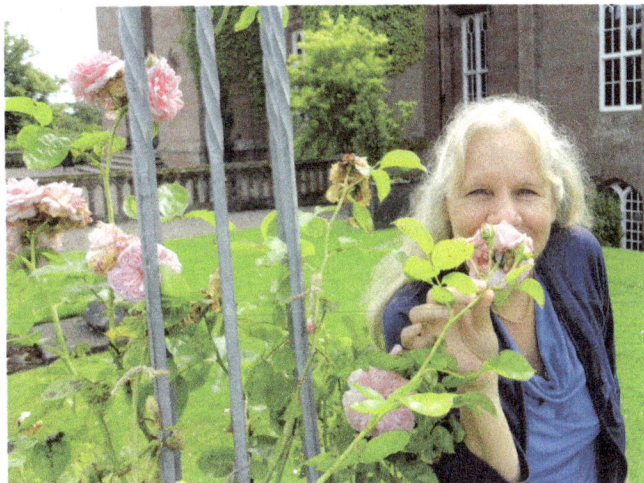

*"Beauty is vain: but a woman that feareth the Lord,
she shall be praised." (Proverbs 31:30)*

PART VII

Death's Painful Separation

In Frames and Cells

Fondest memories flooding back
Birthday party celebrating
Embracing warmth in that day packed
Every heart participating.

This present pain piercing my soul
Yesterday…no, never again
Please, could you just come back once more
Jump and embrace me from that frame?

Impossible, remain in there
I'll change the frame into a cell
When my guard's down and unaware
Another death I'll die and bear.

But, through the fog, my heart perceives
That frames and cells will disappear
In resurrection, I believe
Inseparable…gone deaths and tears.

Hope, this whispers…someday may I
Focus through frames with faded scars?
Tinted with faith, hinting clear skies
Sweet memories that jump through bars!

*"If in this life only we have hope in Christ,
we are of all men most miserable"
(I Corinthians 15:19)*

Sweeping Your Dust with Tears

Asleep in Jesus, sweet deep peace
But my heart bleeds and my soul weeps
Turmoil for you, struggles, defeat?
All vanished with your last heartbeat.

Salty dreaming in my coffee
Misplaced—away—temporary?
No, I don't see you reappear
Denied denials, caffeine clear.

Years and years, the wound keeps oozing
Birthdays, holidays, undoing
"If only" portraits…might have been
On my heart's canvas, smeared within.

Struggling to brush away the dust
That's building upon all your stuff
Compare and sweep lost years with tears…
Forever with twenty-eight years!

(David) said, "can I bring him back again?
I shall go to him, but he shall not return to me"
(II Samuel 12:23)

Riverside Memorial Gardens

Your father visited today
Forgive me that I did not too
Do not deduce I missed this date
I'm feeling weary weather-blue.

Close, in the neighborhood, I know
He placed those plastic ones again
Real ones wither, there nothing grows
But, pain and weeds from teary rain.

Asking Jesus all about you
A casket can't contain your soul
It hurts the confirmation true
Spheres from me, not six feet lower.

We'll both be startled by the shout
Forever joined, no more bereaved
Bid good riddance, gloomy hideout
Fly to heaven, this graveyard leave!

"For the Lord himself shall descend from heaven
with a shout…and the dead in Christ shall rise first:
Then we which are alive and remain shall be caught
up together with them…and so shall we ever be with the Lord"
(I Thessalonians 4:16, 17)

The Heavenly Bedroom

Four loved ones passed in four short years
Departure bled my heart with tears
My parents' bodies, expired, old
Souls longing for heaven's threshold.

My sister, blooming, full of life
A daughter, mother, friend and wife
Not scheduled to leave so soon
When petals dropped seemed only noon.

Our dear son's death made our hearts bleed
Heart-wrenching question, *"Must he leave?"*
A kidnapping that left us numb
The nightmare we're still reeling from.

Jesus gently led them upstairs
A special bedroom, deceased share
Tenderly tucking them in bed
"Your work is over, rest", He said.

In His presence, they peaceful sleep
Disturbed by nothing, sleep so deep
Enjoying Jesus, safely home
Dead, lifeless bodies in their tombs.

Their sleep will cease. They will awake
When Christ returns, His church to take
Angelic voice, with trumpet blast
Shatter the silence, nap won't last.

Graves will open, bodies be changed
Such immortal blessed exchange!
Up to the clouds quickly, they'll fly!
With joy, we'll join them in the sky!

Reunited to never part
Comforting hope, consoling heart!
Life rushes on and I must serve
Cherished reunion, there reserved.

"Concerning them which are asleep, that ye sorrow not
"even as others" which have no hope" (I Thess 4:13)

Martha, Mary and Me

Two sisters said exact same words
But, Jesus heard two different tones
Martha asked, *"Why?"* Mary said, *"Lord!"*
With both of them He shared his soul.

Like Martha, I at first asked, *"Why?"*
Then, Jesus swept tears from his eyes
Like Mary now it's *"Lord"*, I cry
Though still with questions mystified.

"Lord if thou hadst been here, my brother had not died"
(John 11:21,32)

A Tender Tissue for our Tears

Somewhere just like here, the city of Nain
When God gave great blessings, then took away
To her and to me, a place of deep pain
Shadowy valley of dreaded dismay.

Déjà vu filling her sad, soggy mind
Never in foggiest—who she would meet
None but the Prince of Life, Jesus, disguised
Said to this widow and mother, *"don't weep!"*

In secret concert with motherly souls
Love flowing there, heart to hand, through to bier
Her tears to drain and her sorrow console
Bright light illuminate death's dreary sphere.

Into invisible world of the dead
His powerful voice commanded, *"Arise!"*
Shredding death's garments for new life instead
Can you imagine her joyful surprise?

I, too heard your whisper, *"Sweetest, don't weep"*
I, too sensed your presence, nigh to my side
*"I'm watching your young man, mother, he sleeps
With just a nudge, he'll arise, glorified!"*

*In heaven, I'll place him in your embrace
Lonesome mother from child, never to part."*
My Lord Jesus Christ praise for special grace
Compassion to heal aching mothers' hearts.

*"And when the Lord saw her, he had compassion
on her, and said unto her, "Weep not". (Luke 7:13)*

PART VIII

Bitter Anguish through Fiery Trials

Strings in the Willow

As weeping willow stoops my soul
my soggy hair hangs limp and sags
the tears just gush, joining below
this graveyard stream that juts and jags.

So painfully the branches sway
in lazy breezes as they sweep
the salty bank of sorrow gray
turns murky mud, the more I weep.

This separation gnaws and tears
a gaping, oozing open sore
a hollow churning gut despair
my aching heart smarts to the core.

The harp's been flung high, far up top
perhaps a whisper to the strings?
a nudge unprop, a push to drop
suggestion, stirring…song to bring

A touch that plucks strings a little
blending pain and praise together
rippling, mingling with the river
just to trust ahead gets better!

Such tender hugs of comfort, love
hope infiltrating through the dark
embracing arms of God above
so slowly lifting up my heart.

"By the rivers of Babylon…we wept…
we hanged our harps upon the willows"
(Psalms 137: 1,2)

Therapy from Calvary

The fragrant breezes that blow from the cross
like healing ointment on injuries, loss.
Just think of Jesus, so gentle and kind
on Calvary's cross, surrendered, confined.

The vicious malice that He there endured
as shame and mocking was on Him unfurled.
Suffering tenderness, unselfish one
accentuating sacrificial love.

Meditating the grace—yes, He restrained
Angelic myriads under his reign.
With heart-broken tears, He would persevere
his wails reverberate over the years.

While He was suffering, anguishing, there
his bleeding heart interceded in prayer.
Any revenge to God was submitted
all in to honor his Father's mission.

Lord, when my wounds are secreting and sore
firmly compress, so they smolder no more.
Bandage my damaged soul and dry my tears
press close to your heart and quiet my fears!

"With his stripes we are healed." (Isaiah 53:5)

Dropping Petals from a Cascading Vine

I really strive to find my smile
no one likes a gloomy profile
photo just flipped it upside down?
inside selfie—a hopeless frown

For praise, I strain to find my song
warbling birds left, with summer gone
Musician, string my chords again
ripple still harp with some refrain

My skin, has, Doctor, lost its feel
numb, frozen, cold. But, can you heal?
defibrillator charge, restart
to power plug in, reboot heart!

Tears, Comforter, have washed my joy
the party flopped, my life's destroyed
a violent storm shook off the grapes
depression drizzles down my face

My cell phone died, forbidding words
laryngitis buried it inwards
before my mic was strong and clear
now muffled whispers to those near

App disappeared, somewhere, someway
trip's GPS, my trust betrayed
conundrum muddled up my brain
my memory's murky from the rain
Job's thieves robbed me while I sorrowed
stripped me bare and all parts borrowed

Yet Christ's life-blood dripped from his cross
He shared my pain, fragranced my loss
Faded petals, all crushed and torn
pearly heart tears together mourned
off'ring empathy to others
scented, soothing salve for suff'ers

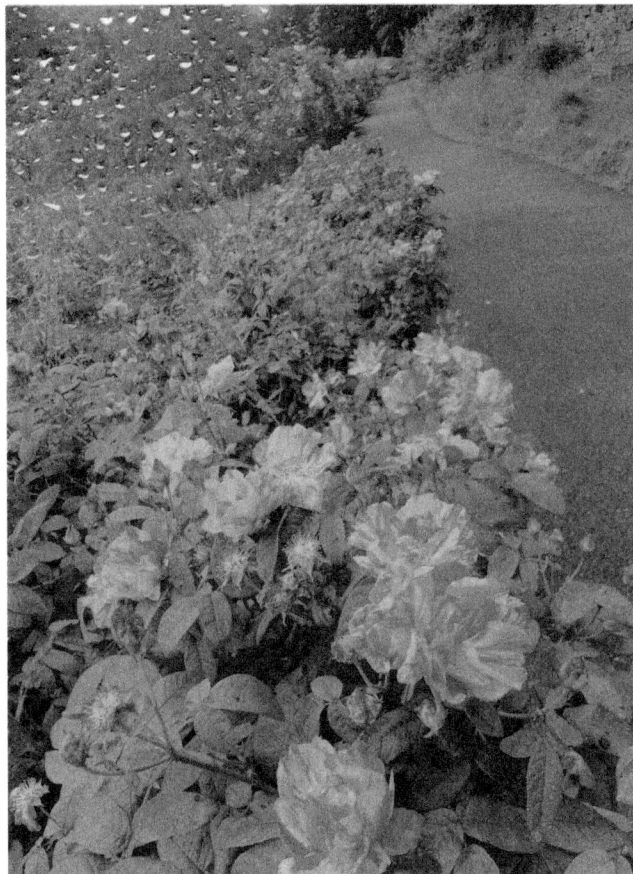

'the God of all comfort; who comforteth us in all our
tribulation, that we may be able to comfort them which
are in any trouble, by the comfort wherewith we ourselves
were comforted of God." (II Corinthians 1: 3, 4)

The Gentle Deliquesce

Offences blast us cold as snow
My Jesus told they would, He knows
He voiced even He'd upset me
Hot tears latent, *"I'm most sorry."*

My Lord foresaw today's sorrow
But didn't sweeten to less sour
He hears my hurts with tender hush
Confiding love thaws by its touch!

Someday the mystery will be solved
Each why explained, each pain involved
Then valued how his plan evolved
For now, draw close, the ice dissolve!

"Then Jesus answering said unto them…
Blessed is he, whosoever shall not be
offended in me." (Luke 7:22, 23)

Golden Embers

Brittle dry sticks, green once, earning
Copious Eshcol's harvest store
Gardener pruned, started the burning
Friction, ignition, kindle, roar.

Scorching, sizzling, scalding, searing
Pleas for mercy in dire distress
Scissors cutting, ripping, tearing
Fiery tongues reach to possess.

Center ground towers another
Strongly supporting, three and me
Lover, Intercessor, Conqueror
Never forsaken—only cleave!

Red with ashes, testing rages
Predetermined, my Lord's heart knows
Temps and phases of the furnace
When finished, embers glisten gold!

"the trial of your faith, being much more
precious than of gold that perisheth, though
it be tried with fire, might be found unto
praise and honour and glory…of Jesus Christ."
(I Peter 1:7)

PART IX

Hopeful Encouragement and Inspiration

Good, Great, Best!

"They're starved and parched," the shepherd said
To sweet green pastures, his fold led
Then from the cool brook they all lapped
Their shepherd happy on the bank.

"He'll self-destruct," the shepherd gasped
Around lamb's head, the rod crook clasped
To safely pull it from the cliff
Before it slips over th'abyss.

"Their hearts are crushed," the shepherd wept
Felt empathy in valley, death
Behind the shadow flickers light
Where tears won't flow, exists no night.

"Lonely, depressed," the shepherd groaned
In bleakest wilderness, there host
A feast of joyful fellowship
Cheerful singing, streaming worship!

"They're all hell-bound," the shepherd sighed
Had shed his precious blood and died
Prepared a mansion for their rest
Our awesome Shepherd! Good, Great, Best!

"The Lord is my shepherd: I shall not want." (Psalm 23:1)

Communion's Secret Fortress

In our secret place, Lord Jesus
On a ledge of refuge fortress
Hidden by your hand's cool shadow
Light beams break through old scarred nail holes!

Securely quiet, here I rest
Bird, cuddled softly in her nest
Outside the storm howls on, prolonged
In my heart, your soothing love song.

Because for me, you bore the storm
Exposed, bare on this earth's platform
Every force amassed against you
Satan and man, Holy God too!

Glorious conqueror for me
Love's deepest, all pervading peace
Precious confidences sharing
Resting, in your strength unfailing.

Safely soon in heaven's haven
Grasp your hands, where my name's graven
There enhancing my affections
Through afflictions…your protection!

*"He that dwelleth in the secret place
of the most High, shall abide under the shadow
of the Almighty." (Psalm 91:1)*

Natural and Spiritual Serotonin

To ho-hum meal, add side of cheer
Squirt joy in lukewarm coffee, dear
Splash beauty on the ugly grey
Lift shades of gloom for sunshine's rays!

Get-up-and-go pour in drained tank
Deposit cash in empty bank
At animal's fun antics laugh
And chuckle at your photograph!

Heaven's bread from oven, hotter
Frosted glass of living water
Heart-written script from King of Love
My personal soul coach above.

Full vaults and vaults of God's riches
Present, future, rainbow blessings
Mansion reserved of wooing rooms
Streaming lyrical worship tunes.

Thanksgiving transforms dark blue moods
Praise raises depressed attitudes
Forever treasured by my Lord
My shield, exceeding great reward!

"Why art thou cast down, O my soul?…
Hope thou in God: for I shall yet praise him
who is the health of my countenance," (Psalm 43:5)

Not Much, But Mine for Him

Through all my life, strive for a crown
To cast at Jesus' nail scarred feet
Nothing allow this goal defeat
Or anyone to tear it down.

Discouragement will not derail
Inspired, my spirit by the goal
God's love will fortify my soul
Beyond the storms, support my sail.

This busy life, cluttered with stuff
And challenged by relationships
Sorrows, temptations and hardships
Distract me? Really, that's enough?

I love my Savior's blessed feet
They led him to a cross of shame
For me He suffered unknown pain
Salvation gained, for me, complete.

Empty-handed? Radiant gems!
To reflect his awesome glory
Purpose for my life's short story
The quest to gather these for him.

*"Behold, I come quickly: hold that fast which thou hast,
that no man take thy crown." (Revelation 3:11)*

PART X

Perspectives on Present-Day Issues

Creative Designer or... Evolution?

Voice activated, illumed light
God spoke, light sparked, displaced the night!
Chemist figured liquid—water
Poured it into ocean pockets.

Farmer blended thick, rich dark dirt
Valleys, hills formed, mountains, hence…earth!
Delicious fruit trees just sprung up
Bulging fruit cheeks—seeds in their cups!
Stunning flowers, jewels blooming
Fragranced with a pinch of perfume.

Moon and stars popped off his fingers!
In the night sky, watch them flicker
Nine spinning planets hung in space!
Timely rotated in their place.
This red fire ball enflamed the sky!
Without its warmth, we all would die
Too close, we'd torch into fried corpse
Earth orbits sun. Moon orbits us!

God's hands fastened fins on fishes
Produced the slimy things that swish
On the birds, he pinned soft feathers
Weightlessly they soar the heavens!
Strung in tiny throats, their shrill songs
They praise Him, warbling, all day long!

Kingdoms of animals, planned zoo
Vibrantly symbiotic too
Bright stripes, pop spots, jumping, running
What variety! Some—funny!

Brilliant potter with mud comprised
Engineered man, his choicest prize!
Then to connect us to God, whole
Deposited immortal soul.

We marvel, praise and we adore
Ingenius beauty outpoured!
Implausible…perceptive folks
Blinded by evolution's joke!

*"For the invisible things of him from the creation
of the world are clearly seen, being understood
by the things that are made, even his eternal power
and Godhead; so that they are without excuse:"*
(Romans 1:20)

Safe Baby Harbor

Envision Jewish mothers' angst…
Pharaoh and Herod—wicked kings
Tiny dead bodies on Nile's bank
Baby's spilled blood…Horror begins!

Today, the infants try to cry
But, mother's choice drowns out their pleas
Their right to life has been denied
The womb, a tomb? Culture agrees.

The tender shepherd clutched his sheep
Discarded, hurled from this earth's shores
Arrested from abortion's heap
For heaven's nursery of joy!

Foster family together
Millions in their baby booties
Nightmares or fears or tears? Never!
Nurtured by angelic nannies.

Can you not hear their darling squeals?
Happy, healthy, loved and treasured
Jesus' jewels, tumbling cartwheels
Safely home, forever pampered!

"Thou hast covered me in my mother's womb…
My substance was not hid from thee, when I was made in secret…
Thine eyes did see my substance, yet being unperfect;
and in thy book all my members were written,
which in continuance were fashioned, when as yet there was none of them."
(Psalm 139: 13, 15, 16)

Voiceless Victims

Where are they—tongue-tied, without voice
People forbidden to rejoice?
They're underground, but can be found
Down-trodden victims (mum's their sound!)

Dear unborn babies in the womb
Nurturing nest now changed to tomb
Sweetest, innocent, tiny voice
Muzzled by mother's selfish choice.

Scared children from parents kidnapped
By heartless criminals entrapped
Or human traffickers, enchained
Traumatized but, they can't complain.

Genocide forced homeless races
Exiled from their habitations
Refugee camps, hungry, dirty
Infants, children… dying early.

Preys of domestic violence
Treated like a useless nuisance
Families plagued, substance abuse
Women and children, trapped and bruised.

Dear Lord, these dear ones dare not talk
Open your door, we humbly knock
On their behalf, please intercede
Oppression end. Oh, set them free!

Gift them with this intuition
You're near in their situation
Loving them and you understand
Because from earth, you too were banned.

You suffered on the cruel cross
To save them from eternal loss
You shed your sacred, holy blood
To save and cleanse them from sins' flood.

Soon, you'll come back, perhaps today
Snatch up your church and whisk away!
Please reach these precious, silenced ones
Adopt them your—daughters and sons!

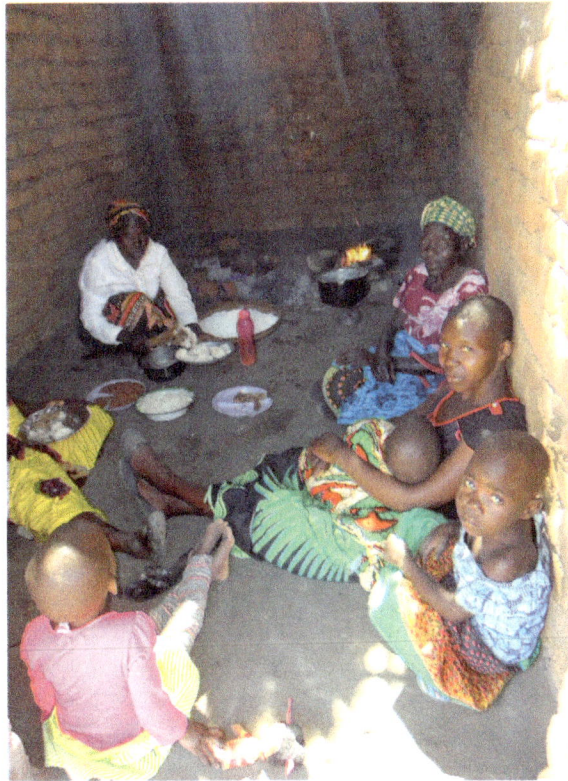

"God is our refuge and strength, a very present help in trouble."
(Psalm 46:1)

115

The Bible's Thirteenth Step

Here's a hug, friend, sit on the couch
I'd like to help you with your life
Reasons, actions, fallouts, about—
Questions, suggestions through the strife.

Explain to me about your pain
Sorrowful heartaches, hollow soul
Self-esteem, respect's been all drained
Phony friends and families' toll.

Repeatedly, you tried and failed
Throwing your life up in the air
Despaired, done in, well you just bailed
Self-destructing, *"who really cares?"*

Satan, hater, devalued you
Alcohol, drugs—those duping tools
Destructively, your mind unscrewed
Manipulating puppet you.

Later, but not much, did the debts…
Jobless, homeless, trust all busted
Loving relatives, friends—upset
Damage, after-math, resulted!

Who put the poison in your mouth?
Who chose to party unrestrained?
Who gave up when all went down south?
How the truth hurts! I feel your pain!

Repentance pulls the sting from shame
Forgiveness—love-wrapped gift from God
Undeserved, free, wonderful grace
Salvation take, thankful to God!

"Jesus forgives me!" shout it loud
God, heaven's judge has been appeased
Lord Jesus Christ, your higher power
For victory, He holds the key!

Two natures now within us lives
Old rotten one remains sinful
New, produces fresh objectives
SOBRIETY'S ACHIEVABLE!

Thirsts and triggers will tantalize
They can't excite the nature **new**
Treat the **old** nature like it died
Dead lifeless dog can't bother you!

Support groups, fellowship with friends
Persist and know you're not alone
Relapse? Don't go to that dead end…
Redial your contacts on your phone.

Jesus, your Lord, gives solid strength
Enjoy your Bible and don't cease
Oceans of love, no depth or length
At two am, sense God's real peace!

"Reckon (consider) ye also yourselves to be
dead indeed unto sin, but alive unto God
through Jesus Christ our Lord".
(Romans 6:11)

Malala's Half Smile

Malala's smile seems half erased
Smart valiant girl from Pakistan
Jihadists bombed her school, defaced
Sunnis or Shias?—Taliban.

Malala treasures her Quran
Prefers the peaceful portions more
Reads, "no compulsion in Islam"*
Like million others, shore to shore.

But, Qutb, Omar and Bin Laden
Read, breathed and slept the same Quran
"Kill unbeliever,"** the Christians
Closely obey Allah's command.

Malala's face shines with two sides
Religious Islam does the same
One with a passive pleasant smile
Other—strained by violent hate.

But both need Jesus, God's dear Son
Who won by death's defeat and lives
His conqu'ring sword's not force, but love
Instead of killing, He forgives!

(* Sura 2:190-94 in the Quran)
(**Sura 2:256 in the Quran)

Shifting Stages

Global players on stage today
From many cultures, countries strong
Foundations shifting, cracking clay
Most dominant, but not for long.

God's Moses toppled Pharaoh's crown
Curious plagues ensuing round
Egyptian dominance was drowned
Oppression over, freedom found.

Lord Jesus came when Romans ruled
Babylon, Persia, Greeks before
Messiah, refused, ridiculled
Crucified—God's only Savior.

History tells its bloody tale
Hateful Hitlers, Sudan Husseins
Power-hungry hearts exposed there
Oppression, terrorism—insane!

Try understanding changing times
Of Daniel's dream, only the feet—
Discernment, prophecies and signs
Ten wiggling toes, almost complete.

Moral decay, dismay abounds
God's stone comes rolling down the stage
Our ears bend upward for the shout
Hebrew schedule, then back on page.

Why should we worry or feel stressed?
Temp'ral will vanish in thin air
Rapture imminent—We rest blessed
Heaven's prepared…Jesus reigns there!

*"The God of heaven shall set up a kingdom, which shall
never be destroyed: and the kingdom shall not be left
to other people, but it shall break in pieces and consume
all these kingdoms, and it shall stand for ever." (Daniel 2:44)*

PART XI

Life's Fleeting Beauty

The Canvas of Life

The artist picked his brush and plan
as sunbeams stretched to touch the land
then, blinking, flickering, one peeked
o'er the horizon half asleep.

The ultra-sound detected shape
the nervous couple hid the tape
her bulging belly bump, it showed
eyes, hopeful and cheeks, rosy glowed.

Pop up! The sun greeted the day…
a big orange ball rising to play
like tiny babe ripe from the womb
new, wet with dew, ready to bloom
with kicks and squeals and squinting eyes
bundled surprise…a new sunrise!

Hear chirping birds as morning yawns
hear toddlers slurrp with sippy straws
in diapers tumbling, try to walk
they jibber jabber, try to talk.

Cell phones—kids—computer whizzes
Sunday school teachings and quizzes
sports teams, education, good friends
disciplines outside the bookends.

Hormones attack…adolescence!
Graduation and acceptance
flashy sports cars, independence
rose-scented, romantic fragrance.

Grown-ups juggle multiple loads
careers and missions…in-prime goals
marriage yields rich fam'ly blessings
high-lights in the landscape, etching.

How fleetingly…love, laugh and cry
as hours, days, years, seasons fly
stored memories in photos, hearts
both charm and sadness, some impart.

White snow's falling, retirement's tired
those golden years no more desired
the heavy ball begins to drop
mere medicine can't make it stop.

The painter dabs his brush, just then
tones touch the canvas once again
dark low-lights captured through the sky
thin sinking circle whispers, *"bye!"*
From heart to hand, his passions flowed
God's masterpiece—God's glory glows!

Perhaps it's morning or at noon
but, never too late, nor too soon
sand from the hour glass has gone
the tale's been told, the portrait's done.
Heart strings tugging, but we can't stay…
our Lover calls! We fly away!
Angelic welcome lines the shore
to usher us through heaven's door!

Our Lord then pitches time away…
a picture-perfect, endless day!

*"He hath made everything beautiful
in his time." (Ecclesiastes 3:11)*

About the Author

Irene was born and raised in a Christian home in Ontario, Canada. She and her husband, Paul have lived and reared their family in Florida, for the last forty years. They started and have enjoyed a small outreach Sunday School for urban kids in West Palm Beach, for the last thirty-two years. In four consecutive years, Irene painfully experienced the physical death of four close family members, which pulls her heart heavenward, as she anticipates reunion with them at the Lord's return.